Simply Sourdough

A Foolproof Beginner's Guide to Delicious Bread, with Step-by-Step Instructions Anyone Can Master

Kate Baker

McGilvray Press

Copyright © 2025 by Kate Baker

This is the revised and expanded second edition of Simply Sourdough – A Foolproof Beginner's Guide to Delicious Bread, with Step-by-Step Instructions Anyone Can Master, originally published in 2024 under the name Kate McGilvray. This edition includes updated instructions, new recipes, additional guidance for beginner bakers and refinements based on reader feedback.

All rights reserved. No part of this publication may be reproduced, stored or transmitted in any form or by any means, electronic, mechanical, photocopying, recording, scanning, or otherwise without written permission from the publisher. It is illegal to copy this book, post it to a website, or distribute it by any other means without permission.

Kate Baker asserts the moral right to be identified as the author of this work.

Kate Baker has no responsibility for the persistence or accuracy of URLs for external or third-party Internet Websites referred to in this publication and does not guarantee that any content on such Websites is, or will remain, accurate or appropriate.

Designations used by companies to distinguish their products are often claimed as trademarks. All brand names and product names used in this book and on its cover are trade names, service marks, trademarks and registered trademarks of their respective owners. The publishers and the book are not associated with any product or vendor mentioned in this book. None of the companies referenced within the book have endorsed the book.

Contents

Introduction   1

1. The Tools You'll Need   4
2. Your Starter: a Step-by-Step Guide   11
   The Essential Ingredient
3. Mix, Rest, Stretch & Fold   22
   The Foundation of a Great Loaf
4. Bulk Fermentation   27
   The Waiting Game
5. Shaping the Dough   29
   Easy Does It
6. Proofing   31
   The Final Rest Before the Big Show
7. Ready for the Oven   33
8. Baking the Bread   39
   You're Almost There!

9. Making It Your Own	42
Inclusions, Flavours & Personal Touches	
10. Level Up Your Loaf	47
The Only Limit is Your Imagination!	
11. Sourdough Discard Ideas	53
Delicious Ways to Waste Less	
12. Troubleshooting	60
Common Issues & Quick Reference Guide	
13. Conclusion	64
About the Author	69

Introduction

Welcome (back) to the wonderful world of sourdough bread making!

Whether you're totally new to baking or you've already tried your hand at a few loaves, sourdough is something truly special. It's about using natural ingredients, patience, and a little bit of magic from your starter. It's also about slowing down, tuning in, and creating something nourishing from scratch, something with character, flavour, and heart.

When I first wrote *Simply Sourdough*, I wanted to share a straightforward, beginner-friendly guide that skipped the intimidation and embraced the learning curve. Since then, I've heard from so many readers who've baked their first successful loaf, discovered new confidence in the kitchen, or found a calm, steady rhythm in the process of baking bread. It's been a joy and an honour to be part of that journey.

This revised and expanded second edition includes even more to support you:

-A brand-new chapter on **inclusions and mix-ins**—think seeds, herbs, cheese, fruit, and flavour-packed combinations to make each loaf your own.

-Several **sourdough discard recipes** that turn your leftovers into pancakes, crackers, banana bread, and more.

-Expanded tips, extra guidance, and refinements based on things I've learned (and baked!) since the first edition.

For those who don't know me yet: I came to sourdough later in life, after retiring from more than two decades in law enforcement. Through years of high stress and complex emotional weight, cooking was my refuge; my way to decompress and care for myself and those I love. That became even more important after I was diagnosed with a serious autoimmune condition, and I made the choice to significantly reduce processed sugar, dairy, and gluten in my diet.

While sourdough obviously still contains gluten, I've found that the slow fermentation, lack of additives, and ability to control what goes into my bread has made a world of difference for my gut health, and my overall wellbeing.

Like many people, I used to think sourdough was too technical for someone like me. I'm more of an instinctive cook than a recipe-follower, and I figured it was too fussy, too precise. But I gave it a try, and then another, and slowly, loaf by loaf, I found my rhythm. It wasn't about perfection. It was about learning. About curiosity. And about being okay with a wonky crust or even a complete failure here and there!

This guide is everything I wish I'd had when I was beginning my sourdough journey. It may seem at first like a LOT of steps, but when you're starting out, I want you to have clear, simple step-by-step instructions, approachable advice, and the encouragement to keep going when things don't turn out quite right. You don't need fancy equipment or professional skills, just a bit of patience, a sense of adventure, and maybe don't mind a bit of flour in your eyebrows.

So let's get started. Your first loaf is waiting, and I can't wait to see what you create.

The Tools You'll Need

Before diving in, let's make sure you have everything you need. Don't worry, you don't need a lot of fancy gear to make delicious sourdough bread, and it can all be sourced from your local homewares retailer, or online, for a very reasonable price.

You absolutely do not need a high-end cast iron bread pan costing hundreds of dollars to get amazing results. I started with a $25 cast iron Dutch oven from Target that's still the one I use the most, to this day! You probably already have, or can find an alternative for most of the tools you need, so don't get hung up on having the "right" ones. Just dive in!

Here's a list of the essentials:

Mixing Bowls - You'll need at least two large mixing bowls for mixing and proofing the dough. I like to use a Pyrex or other microwave proof bowl to warm the water before mixing in my starter.

A container for your starter – Get yourself a couple of glass jars or containers, one with a volume of about 500ml / 18oz , and one about 1000ml / 36oz. I generally use the smaller of these two, but when first creating your starter you might need one with a bit more room. I like to use a wide mouth mason jar so I can take some cheesecloth and use the outer screw lid to hold it in place, but there are plenty of alternatives, probably in your kitchen cupboard right now! I stick with the same one because it has a nice wide mouth, which makes it easier for adding and incorporating the flour, as well as scraping down the sides. It's best to have a container you can see through so you can monitor your starter activity from all angles.

Digital Scale - Weighing your ingredients gives you the best results. This is true of any recipe, in my opinion – I always look for online recipes that have a metric/imperial conversion option. Trust me, it's more reliable than measuring cups, especially if you're using recipes from different countries.

Bench Scraper - This handy tool helps you move dough around, scrape it off surfaces, and shape it. I use both silicone and steel ones for different tasks now, but just a regular plastic one will get the job done, as it did for me when I got started.

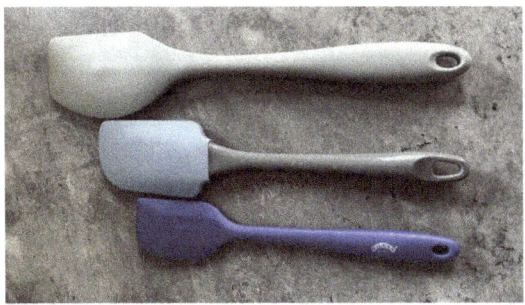

Silicone spatula – I use these in just about all areas of my cooking. I think I have about ten of them in different sizes and levels of flexibility, it's such a great all-round tool!

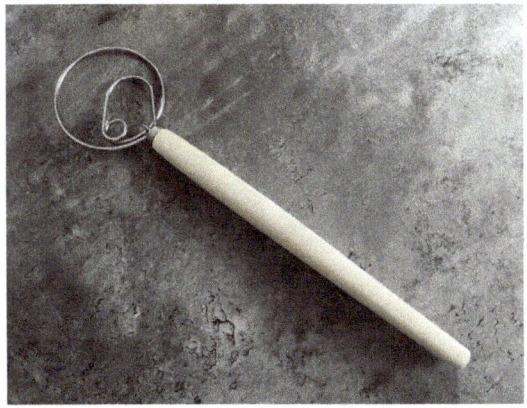

Danish Dough Whisk – this tool, also known as a *brodpisker* (unsurprisingly, the Danish word for "bread whisk"), is a special mixing tool with a long wooden handle and a strong wire coil on one end that makes it super effective at mixing bread dough. This is not essential, but I find it really helps in that initial dough-mixing stage, and it works better than a wooden spoon or normal whisk for the task.

Banneton (Proofing Basket) - This helps your dough hold its shape while it proofs. If you don't have one, a regular bowl will work. You can use cheesecloth, a tea towel or cloth napkin to line it with so the dough doesn't stick to the sides, but a lot of home cooks just dust liberally with rice flour and also get great results!

Dutch Oven - This helps create a steamy environment that gives sourdough its amazing crust. You can also use a baking stone and a tray of water if you don't have a Dutch oven.

THE TOOLS YOU'LL NEED

Razor Blade or Lame (pronounced "lah-may") - This is used to score your dough before baking. It allows the bread to expand properly in the oven. A sharp knife works too, but it must be VERY sharp. If it's not, all you're going to do is drag and tear the dough!

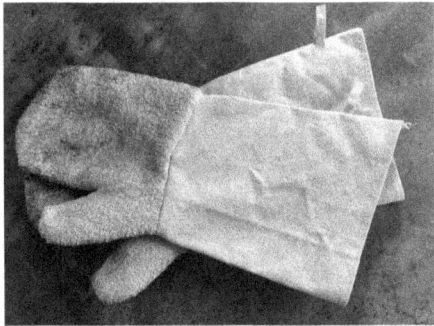

Baking gloves – Get yourself some long, high-temperature baking gloves for safety. We are working at a very high temperature when baking the sourdough, and you need to protect not just your hands but your lower arms, too. Trust me, I learned this the hard way (and still have the scars to remind me!)

Having these tools will make your sourdough journey easier, but if you don't have them all, don't worry—there are always creative alternatives.

Let's move on to the fun part!

Your Starter: a Step-by-Step Guide

The Essential Ingredient

Your sourdough starter is the heart of the entire process. This starter is what gives sourdough its signature flavour and rise.

Creating a sourdough starter is like inviting a little magic into your kitchen. With just flour, water, and a bit of patience, you can capture wild yeast and good bacteria from the air to help your bread rise and give it that delicious tangy flavour. The process takes about a week, depending on your climate and ambient temperature, and with some love and care, you'll have a starter that you can use for years to come.

Mine is nearly three years old now, which is juvenile compared to others, but I'm very proud of her, and she makes an amazing loaf every time!

What You'll Need

- Whole wheat flour (to start with)

- All-purpose flour (for later)

- Water (preferably filtered or non-chlorinated – I use filtered water)

- A glass jar or container (a 500ml/18oz to 1000ml/36oz, wide-mouth jar is preferable to make it easy to mix and leave room for the starter to grow)

- A scale or measuring cups (a digital scale is my preference)

- A spoon or spatula

- A clean cloth or paper towel to cover the jar (I use a piece of cheesecloth and a rubber band)

- An extra rubber band, or some tape you can write on (to mark where your starter is before it rises)

Step 1: Day One - The Beginning

1. Combine Flour and Water

In a glass jar or container, combine 60 grams (about ½ cup) of whole wheat flour with 60 grams (about ¼ cup) of water. Whole wheat flour is best to start with because it has more nutrients that wild yeast love, but it's not essential. You want to use a plain all-purpose flour that has at least 12% protein content – check the nutrition panel on the package. The higher the protein percentage the better. The extra gluten strength the higher protein supports will give you a stronger starter and ultimately a more resilient dough.[1]

2. Mix It Up

Use a spoon or spatula to mix until you have a thick, smooth paste. Make sure all the flour is hydrated, and there are no dry spots left. The consistency should resemble a thick batter or pancake mix.

3. Cover and Wait

Cover the jar loosely with a clean cloth or paper towel to keep dust out while still allowing airflow. I have used a lot of different covers; cheesecloth, a loosely fitted lid, a mesh insert – just use whatever you've got that will allow the starter to breathe to prevent pressure from building up. Leave the jar at room temperature, ideally between 21°C to 24°C (70°F and 75°F). Now, we wait for the magic to begin!

Step 2: Day Two - Check-In and Feed

1. Check for Bubbles

On day two, you might not see much action yet, but it's still good to check. Look for any bubbles, which are a sign that wild yeast is starting to work. If you see bubbles, that's great! If not, don't worry - it can take some time.

2. Add Flour and Water

To feed your starter, add 60 grams of whole wheat flour and 60 grams of water. Stir well to incorporate everything. You should see that thick paste again after mixing.

3. Cover and Wait Again

Cover the jar and leave it at room temperature for another 24 hours.

---

1. https://cookgeeks.net/bread-flour-vs-high-protein-flour/

Step 3: Day Three - More Signs of Life

1. Look for Changes

By day three, you should start to see more bubbles and perhaps even some expansion. You might notice a tangy, slightly sour smell—this is the wild yeast and bacteria starting to do their work.

2. Switch to All-Purpose Flour

Now that things are starting to happen, you can switch to using all-purpose flour. Add 60 grams of flour and 60 grams of water to the jar. Stir well and scrape down the sides.

3. Mark the Level

You can use a rubber band or piece of tape to mark the level of your starter. This helps you see if it's rising, which means it's getting stronger.

Step 4: Day Four - Feeding Time

1. Notice More Bubbles and Activity

Today, you should see even more bubbles and maybe some significant growth. The starter might have a stronger sour smell, which is normal.

2. Discard and Feed

By now our starter volume is getting pretty large, so remove and dispose of up to three-quarters of the starter. Discarding helps control the growth and keep your starter from getting too large. As you progress you might want to use this discard for other recipes (see some ideas in chapter 13!), but at this point you're really focusing on creating a nice, strong starter. DO NOT PUT IT DOWN YOUR DRAIN! It's not great for your plumbing OR the environment.

After discarding, feed your starter with 60 grams of all-purpose flour and 60 grams of water. Mix well and leave it at room temperature.

Step 5: Days Five to Seven - Growing Stronger

1. Continue Daily Feedings

Each day from now on, repeat the same process: discard half of the starter and add 60 grams of all-purpose flour and 60 grams of water. Stir well and cover it again.

2. Check for Activity

By day five or six, you should see your starter increasing in size within 6-8 hours after feeding. This means the wild yeast is active and thriving.

3. Bubbles and Smell

Your starter should have a lot of bubbles and a pleasant, slightly sour smell by now. If your starter doesn't appears as active as you hoped at this stage, don't worry - sometimes it just needs a couple of extra days, depending on the ambient temperature and humidity where you live.

Step 6: Day Seven - Ready to Bake

1. *Am* I ready to bake? How will I know?

By day seven, your starter should be doubling (or more) in size regularly and full of bubbles. Before making bread, always make sure your starter is active. How can you tell? It should be bubbly and it can double or even triple in size after feeding. A trick that many home bakers will swear by is the "float test". The theory is that you take a small spoonful and drop it into a glass of water, and if it floats, you're good to go. *However*, I have found that passing the float test is less "essential" and more "a possible guide".

Somewhere along the line, bakers were told to watch for their starter to *double* as a sign it was ready to use or feed. But doubling is just a number. It's arbitrary. Many healthy starters triple, or even more, and others reach peak activity well before they double.

*What matters isn't **height**. It's **activity**.*

When you're starting out, use the float test so you can begin to learn what a happy and healthy starter looks like. That's certainly what I did! As I've become more confident though, I've found that the float test just isn't the one and only guide it's sometimes cracked up to be. Instead, as you progress, learn to read the signs of peak fermentation. Look *down into the jar*, not just at the side. Here's what to look for:

-A thick layer of bubbles on the surface

-Noticeable ridges and uneven edges around the top

-The sides may start to level off or slide slightly

-A domed surface usually means it's **not** at peak yet (*Though some starters don't dome at all — it depends on the jar and the hydration*)

Don't rely on the starter falling as a sure sign it peaked. Sometimes just removing the lid, tapping the jar, or moving it slightly can cause it to deflate, even if it wasn't at peak yet.

I place a marker on my starter jar purely as a guide, but bubbles, ridges, and fermentation cues tell you far more than a doubling line ever will, and reading these is a skill you'll develop with time. Be patient, with yourself, *and* your fledgling starter!

2. Feeding Schedule

If your starter is ready, you can continue feeding it once a day if you're planning to bake often, or store it in the refrigerator and feed it once a week if you're baking less frequently. After nearly three years, my starter is pretty strong, so I don't need to feed it every day, or even every week! I store it in the refrigerator and only feed it the night before I plan to start my baking process.

Starter, take your mark!

Troubleshooting Tips

No Bubbles? If you're not seeing bubbles, it could be too cold. Try moving your starter to a warmer spot, like near a warm appliance. I advise against putting it in the oven, even on a proofing setting, if you have it. Temperature that's even slightly too high can be lethal to your starter!

Too Sour? If the smell becomes overly sour or unpleasant, you may need to feed it more often or remove less during the discarding step.

Hooch (Liquid on Top) - Sometimes a greyish liquid can form on top of your starter. This is called hooch and means your starter is hungry. Pour off the hooch and feed it as usual.

Maintaining Your Sourdough Starter

Daily Feeding

If kept at room temperature, your starter will need daily feedings. Discard half and feed it with equal parts flour and water.

Refrigeration

To slow it down, keep your starter in the fridge. Feed it once a week by discarding half and adding flour and water.

Using Your Sourdough Starter

Once your starter is active and bubbly, it's ready to be used in bread, pancakes, pizza dough, or any number of other tasty recipes. When baking, take some of the starter to use in your dough, then feed the remaining starter to keep it going. This way, you'll always have a steady supply for baking.

Congratulations!

By following these steps, you've created a living sourdough starter. Your very own wild yeast culture!

Sometimes, your starter might act a little lazy. If it's not rising well or looking sluggish, try giving it more frequent feedings, keeping it warm, or just being patient. Your starter is a living thing, and it's normal for it to have moods.

Now you're ready to bake some amazing sourdough bread and explore all sorts of recipes. It's an adventure that only gets better as your starter matures, and your bread-baking skills improve.

You can also watch my instructional video showing how I feed my starter on my YouTube channel, bakekat kitchen!

Mix, Rest, Stretch & Fold

The Foundation of a Great Loaf

Now that your starter is happy and active, it's time to bring everything together. This is where your dough begins to take shape, both literally and structurally. In this chapter, we'll go through my go-to basic sourdough loaf recipe and the gentle techniques I use to build strength in the dough without traditional kneading.

My Basic Loaf Recipe

Here's the formula I return to time and time again:

500g flour – I use a blend of 400g organic stone-ground white flour and 100g organic spelt flour. You can experiment with your own mix of bread flour and whatever others you have access to. It's so interesting (and delicious) to experiment with different flours, learn their flavour profiles, and what works for you.

400g water – I use filtered water, heated to around 32–34°C (90–93°F) in the microwave.

100g active starter

10g salt

Step 1: Mix and Autolyse

Start by mixing your water and starter in a large bowl. Use a Danish dough whisk if you have one, it's great for incorporating the flour without overworking it. Gradually add the flour, about 100g at a time, stirring until you form a shaggy dough. Don't worry if it looks rough and uneven at this stage; that's exactly what we expect.

Once combined, cover the bowl and let it rest in a warm spot for 30 minutes to an hour. This resting period is called the **autolyse**, and it's a quiet little miracle that does wonders for your dough. During this time, the flour hydrates fully and begins to form gluten strands, which will make the dough more elastic and easier to handle later.

Think of the autolyse as giving your dough a gentle head start. It's an effortless step that can make a big difference in texture and structure.

Step 2: Add the Salt

After the autolyse, it's time to add the salt. DO NOT FORGET THE SALT! You might think, "Surely it can't make *that* much of a difference?", but I promise, your loaf will be pretty much inedible without it. I like to moisten my hands slightly; it helps incorporate the salt more easily without sticking too much or messing with the hydration levels. Don't worry if the dough feels sticky at this point. That's completely normal.

There's no need for an electric mixer here, your hands are more than enough. Gently fold and squish the salt into the dough until it's well integrated. You'll still be able to feel grains of salt at this stage, but don't worry, they'll dissolve as the dough progresses. Once done, cover the bowl again and let it rest for another 30 minutes.

Step 3: Stretch and Fold

Now we move into the stretch and fold phase, which replaces traditional kneading. It's a simple, hands-on way to build strength in your dough while encouraging fermentation and structure. This is not about brute strength, but gently, consistently working the dough for a minute or two, several times over an extended period.

Every 30 minutes over the next 2–3 hours, you'll perform a set of stretch and folds. Here's how:

1. Wet your hands slightly to prevent sticking.

2. Gently lift one side of the dough, stretch it upward, then fold it over onto itself.

3. Rotate the bowl a quarter turn and repeat on all four sides.

4. Cover the dough and let it rest until the next set.

Each time you do this, you'll notice your dough becoming smoother, more elastic, and more cohesive. You're encouraging the gluten network to develop without overworking it.

Don't stress too much about the exact timing. I've learned through experience that sourdough is pretty forgiving. As long as you stay roughly on track and pay attention to how the dough feels, it will guide you.

Step 4: Coil Fold

Another technique I love is the coil fold, which I use every time I bake. It's especially helpful with higher hydration doughs, but works well here too. It's very simple.

1. Gently lift the dough from the center with both hands, letting it stretch downward.

2. Fold the dough under itself, forming a soft coil.

3. Rotate the bowl and repeat until all sides have been folded

For this recipe, I typically do three sets of stretch and folds, followed by two sets of coil folds, each 30 minutes apart. Whether it's the technique or the rhythm of the process, this combination works beautifully for me. My dough is consistently strong, elastic, and easy to shape.

This is the part of the process where I really settle into the rhythm of baking. It's quiet, tactile, and surprisingly calming; just you, your dough, and a few gentle folds that transform a few simple ingredients into something alive and full of promise.

In the next chapter, we'll move into bulk fermentation, where your dough gets its first long rest and rise.

Bulk Fermentation

The Waiting Game

O nce you've finished the stretch and folds, it's time for bulk fermentation. This is when your dough will rest and rise, allowing the yeast and bacteria to do their work.

During bulk fermentation, the dough can roughly double in size, but do NOT be stressed out if it doesn't get to this point. This can take anywhere from 4 to 8 hours, depending on the temperature of your kitchen. Warmer temperatures will speed things up, while cooler temperatures slow it down.

Keep an eye on the dough - you want it to have increased in size, with bubbles forming on the surface. Don't rush this step; bulk fermentation is key to developing flavour.

Here's the thing with bulk fermentation though: in some climates it works well, in others, it's not so predictable. I have found that with the extremes of temperature and humidity we experience where I live, without being refrigerated, my dough can move at a glacial pace, or overproof in the blink of an eye.

Early on I blew up several bakes this way, so now, for my best results, I count my stretch and fold time as my on-the-counter bulk fermentation.

After I complete the stretch and fold process, I rest the dough for another 20 minutes and then, it's on to shaping, into the bannetons, and into the fridge overnight for what's referred to as the cold retard. In this instance, "retard" is used to mean that it slows down the fermentation process, and for me, this time is where my bread develops its signature sourdough flavour; with practice, you'll find what's right for your physical environment, too.

Now it's time to move on to shaping your loaf!

Shaping the Dough

Easy Does It

After bulk fermentation, it's time to shape the dough. First, gently turn the dough out onto a lightly floured surface. Be careful not to deflate it too much - you want to keep all those lovely air bubbles as intact as possible, but again, it's pretty resilient, so don't stress too much here.

To shape a boule (round loaf), gently pull the edges of the dough toward the centre, creating surface tension on the underside. Flip it over, and use your hands to gently rotate it, tucking the edges under until you have a nice, tight round shape. There are countless easy-to-follow videos online, so check them out for guidance if you need a bit of help here – if I could work out how to do it, so can you!

If you prefer a batard (oval loaf), flatten the dough slightly into a rectangle, then fold one side in over the other, creating a bottom, middle and top layer. Then gently but firmly roll the dough into a cylinder, keeping the surface tension consistent as you pull the dough towards you. The key is to create sufficient surface tension so the dough holds its shape while proofing, and provides a smooth, relatively flaw-free surface for effective scoring before it goes in the oven.

Proofing

The Final Rest Before the Big Show

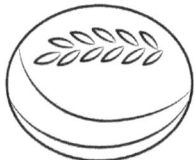

Now that your dough is shaped, it's time for proofing. This is the final rise before baking.

Place your shaped dough into a floured banneton or a bowl lined with a floured tea towel or other cloth. I line my bannetons with cheesecloth, then sprinkle liberally with rice flour to prevent the dough from sticking. Don't use regular flour, as it will absorb moisture and could affect the texture of your loaf. Some people like to put the dough into their bannetons without a liner, but I could never make that work, ending up tearing them as I tried to get them out and wrecking all that great surface tension I'd worked so hard to develop. This resulted in messy loaves which burst in random spots, and although they ended up tasting great, they would look terrible!

I almost always use a "batard" or oval-shaped banneton because I like the slices it produces. A "boule" or round-shaped loaf is still delicious, of course, but I find the inconsistent size of the slices a challenge!

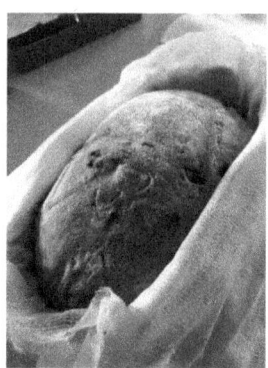

You have two options: proof at room temperature for about 1-2 hours (depending on your ambient temperature), or do a longer, overnight proof in the fridge. This fridge-proof helps develop even more flavour and makes the dough easier to handle when it's time to bake. This is my preference 100% of the time – I find I get more consistent results because the temperature remains constant, something I can't guarantee if it's sitting on the counter in my kitchen. As I mentioned in the last chapter, temperatures where I live can go from as low as zero to 45 degrees Celsius, so I'm not even going to try and make that work!

After placing the dough into the cheesecloth-lined banneton, I fold the remaining cloth over the top, then place the whole thing in a freezer bag which I tie off. You could use a plastic shower cap or something similar. This allows the loaf to continue to prove overnight in the fridge without the top drying out, and the extra cloth folded over the top means any condensation is absorbed before it hits the dough. You'll know your dough is ready to bake when it springs back slowly when gently pressed with a finger, but again, be kind to yourself. This takes a bit of practice!

Ready for the Oven

After your dough has been in the fridge overnight, it's ready for the final step – baking! Preheat your oven to about 245°C (475°F), with your Dutch oven inside. You want it to get to the highest temperature possible before even getting your dough out of the fridge. Keep your oven gloves handy!

Once your oven is up to heat, take your dough from the fridge, remove it from the freezer bag, and uncover the cloth. I take 20cm/8in piece of baking paper which I lay across the top of the dough, and using a flat baking tray on top I turn the loaf out of the banneton and gently remove the cheesecloth.

The strip of baking paper now forms a flap on either side of the long edge of the dough, which you can use as handles to lift the loaf into and out of the Dutch oven. I find it so much easier to place the dough where I need it by doing it this way. Don't try and do this by hand as the dough can lose its shape, and you'll have a pretty good chance of burning yourself (again: I know, because I've done it!)

Time to Score!

Before baking, you'll need to score the dough. Scoring is simply making shallow cuts on the surface of the dough to allow it to expand in a planned way in the oven.

I dust the dough with rice flour before using a razor blade or a lame to make a quick, confident slash across the top of the dough. Make your cuts shallow and swift, so the dough doesn't drag or rip. You can deepen the cut after if you need, but you can't walk it back if you go too far in your first pass. Scoring is both practical and a chance to add a personal touch to your loaf. It can take some practice, though!

Sometimes that bread is going to expand wherever it wants!

I definitely had some random, raggy looking loaves when I first started, but happily it didn't make them taste any less delicious.

Many bakers like to score down the side of the loaf to get what's referred to as an "ear", where the expanding loaf opens up as it bakes. I find this sometimes makes it harder to slice once it's done, so most of the time I score three times across the body of the loaf to maintain an even shape, but this is entirely up to you.

You can keep it simple with a single cut or get creative with patterns – like I said above, this takes practice but even the simplest cuts can look amazing once the loaf comes out of the oven!

Using activated charcoal powder really makes the scoring pop!

Make sure you do score it, though - all that gas created in the fermentation process has to go somewhere, and you want to try and avoid random blowouts all over your loaf! Effective scoring directs the expansion of your loaf in the direction YOU want it to go.

Baking the Bread

You're Almost There!

Before placing the dough into the Dutch oven, I always have a couple of ice cubes ready in a bowl nearby. I like to create extra steam inside to get the best "spring" for my loaf. The extra moisture prevents the crust of the loaf from setting too quickly so it can really pop, giving you a beautiful oven spring and crumb.

Using the "handles" created by the baking paper underneath, carefully lift and place your dough into the preheated Dutch oven, add the ice cubes to the sides (not on top!) cover it with the lid, and pop it in the oven. After 20 minutes, remove the lid and bake for another 20 minutes, until the crust is deep golden brown. Every oven is different though, so remember you'll need to adjust your bake time to suit your equipment.

If you don't have a Dutch oven, you can use a baking stone with an added tray of water in the oven to create steam.

Your bread is done when it sounds hollow when tapped on the bottom or when the internal temperature reaches around 93°C (200°F).

As tempting as it is, let your bread cool for **at least** an hour before slicing. I wait a minimum of six to eight hours before I get anywhere near it with a bread knife! Cooling allows the interior to set properly and enhances the flavour. Slicing too soon can result in a gummy texture, and the loaf can tear.

Once cooled, grab a *sharp* bread knife and cut yourself a slice. Enjoy the fruits of your labour! There's nothing quite like that first bite of fresh, homemade sourdough.

Making It Your Own

Inclusions, Flavours & Personal Touches

One of the things I love most about baking sourdough is how endlessly customizable it is. Once you've mastered your basic loaf, the real fun begins; adding your own flair through inclusions. Seeds, herbs, cheeses, spices, fruits... whatever inspires you can usually find a home in your dough. It's a wonderful way to use up odds and ends from the pantry or fridge, and even better, it makes each loaf feel uniquely yours.

Adding inclusions also means you can turn a standard loaf into something extra special, something that pairs beautifully with soup, makes a sandwich unforgettable, or becomes the kind of breakfast toast you actually look forward to. There's something really satisfying about sharing a loaf that has your own twist to it.

Savoury Add-Ins

Let's start with the savoury. These ingredients can be added during the last few stretch-and-folds, generally after the autolyse and initial mixing are complete, once the dough is beginning to come together and build strength.

Here are some of my favourite savoury inclusions:

Seeds: I love adding whatever I have on hand—pumpkin seeds, linseeds, sunflower seeds, black and white sesame seeds (especially toasted), and hemp seeds all work beautifully. You can mix and match depending on what you've got. I like to keep a "seed blend" jar in the pantry just for this purpose. I add these after the autolyse at the same time as I add the salt.

Flavoured or smoked salts: These can add a real depth of flavour. A little goes a long way. Use them in place of regular salt in your dough, or sprinkle on top just before baking for a dramatic finish.

Herbs: Rosemary is a classic, but thyme, oregano, and even finely chopped sage or parsley can add lovely complexity.

Roasted garlic or caramelised onion: These are rich and fragrant, and they're perfect for folding into your dough. Just make sure they're not too wet. Let them cool and drain a little before adding.

Cheese and cheese alternatives: Shredded hard cheeses like parmesan, pecorino, or a sharp cheddar are brilliant folded in just before shaping. But if you want that umami-rich cheesy flavour without extra moisture, **nutritional yeast** is your friend. I use it often when I want a more delicate loaf that still has a "cheesy" personality.

HOT TIP: When using ingredients with a high moisture or fat content, like berries, cheese or onion, reduce your hydration slightly or pat them dry before adding them in. Your dough will thank you!

Cheesy Bread (Yes, Please!)

One of my go-to comfort bakes is a sharp cheddar and black pepper sourdough. The cheese melts into pockets of rich flavour and the pepper gives it a little kick. For a twist, try adding smoked paprika or chives.

I'll share a full cheesy sourdough loaf recipe in the next section, but if you're dairy-free or just not in the mood for the extra fat and moisture, nutritional yeast gives you that rich flavour with none of the fuss. I usually add 2–3 tablespoons to my flour during mixing for a subtly cheesy loaf that goes great with soups or avocado toast.

Sweet Loaf Ideas

Sweet sourdoughs are underrated, in my opinion. They're the perfect balance of tangy and sweet, and they toast up beautifully. I love playing around with:

Blueberries and cream cheese: Fold in a handful of fresh or frozen blueberries and spoonfuls of cream cheese (not too soft) just before shaping.

HOT TIP: I use dried blueberries for this one, as I don't have to worry about them adversely affecting my hydration levels. I find they absorb just enough moisture from the dough without drying it out, and their structure remains intact whilst still imparting a delicious, subtle flavour throughout the loaf.

Dried fruits: Think raisins, figs, chopped dates, or cranberries. You can soak these for 10–15 minutes in warm water (or orange juice!) first if you like so they don't draw moisture from the dough, but I've found this isn't totally necessary unless the fruits are REALLY dried.

Cinnamon and brown sugar swirl: Roll your dough out after bulk fermentation, spread with a cinnamon-sugar mix, and roll it back up like a jelly roll before final shaping. This is the base of my sourdough cinnamon roll focaccia, which you'll find in the next chapter!

When to Add Inclusions

Here's a general guide:

Inclusion Type	When to Add
Dry seeds/herbs	During final stretch and folds
Wet ingredients	Final fold just before shaping
Delicate ingredients	Gently layered during shaping
Swirls (eg: cinnamon)	Roll in after bulk fermentation

My Philosophy on Mix-Ins

Some people treat sourdough like a delicate science, and that's perfectly okay; I don't believe in gatekeeping in any way. No-one should feel like there's only one "right way" to create anything, because the joy lies in finding our own path. I treat it more like an adventure. If you're curious whether something will work in a loaf, try it! Worst case, you end up with a dud, or an odd but still delicious experiment. In my opinion, failure is the truest teacher. Best case? You discover a new favourite.

In the next chapter, I'll walk you through a few of my go-to flavour-packed bakes, including my sourdough cinnamon roll focaccia—sweet, sticky, and deeply satisfying.

Level Up Your Loaf

The Only Limit is Your Imagination!

Now that we've talked inclusions, let me share two of my absolute favourite recipes—both a little indulgent, both completely worth it. These are the loaves I make when I want to spoil someone (or myself), or when I just need a warm kitchen, a good bake, and a little joy.

Cheesy Sourdough Loaf with Cracked Pepper & Paprika

This loaf is bold, savoury, and deeply satisfying. The sharp cheese melts into little pockets, while the black pepper and paprika give it just enough warmth and depth. It's perfect with soup, amazing for grilled cheese, and makes the best toast you'll ever eat.

Ingredients:

500g bread flour (or 400g bread + 100g spelt)

100g active sourdough starter

370–380g water (slightly lower hydration than your base loaf)

10g smoked salt (or regular sea salt)

1 ½ tsp cracked black pepper

1 tsp smoked paprika (optional, but a non-negotiable for me, I love this stuff!)

120g grated sharp cheddar or vintage tasty cheese

Optional: 2–3 tbsp nutritional yeast for extra depth

Method:

1. **Mix & Autolyse** Mix starter, water, and flour. Let rest for 45–60 minutes.

2. **Add Salt & Spices** Add salt, pepper, paprika, and nutritional yeast (if using). Mix until incorporated.

3. **Stretch & Fold Phase** Perform 3 rounds of stretch and folds, then 2 sets of coil folds every 30 minutes. Add the **cheese** during the **final fold** to prevent it melting or disintegrating into the dough.

4. **Bulk Fermentation** (Now, I skip this step for the reasons previously discussed, but if it works for you, go for it.) Let the dough rise until puffy and roughly doubled (4–6 hours, depending on temperature).

5. **Shape** Gently shape into a boule or batard. Try to fold the

cheese into the centre if it hasn't fully incorporated.

6. **Cold Proof** Place into a banneton, cover, and refrigerate overnight.

7. **Score & Bake** Bake in a preheated Dutch oven at 245°C (475°F), 20 minutes covered, 20 minutes uncovered. Let cool for *at least* an hour before slicing.

I like to mist my dough with a mixture of water and liquid hickory smoke before sprinkling with ground spices like paprika or cumin, or flavoured salt before baking for a golden, flavour-packed crust!

Sourdough Cinnamon Roll Focaccia

This is *pure joy*. It's sticky, fluffy, golden-topped, and impossible to eat just one piece. It also makes a fantastic treat for a deserving friend, family member, neighbour... if you don't eat it all yourself first. I try to have people lined up to gift it to BEFORE I bake it, to save testing my willpower! This is also easy to modify for just about any sweet focaccia, like the Blueberry, Lemon & Almond one I whipped up when I had some leftover starter.

Dough Ingredients:

500g bread flour

100g active sourdough starter

400g water

10g salt

2 tbsp olive oil

Cinnamon Filling:

60g brown sugar (or coconut sugar)

1 tbsp cinnamon

1 tbsp melted coconut oil or vegan butter

Pinch of salt

Optional glaze:

½ cup icing sugar

1 tbsp plant milk

Dash of vanilla

Method:

1. **Mix & Autolyse** Combine starter, water, and flour. Let rest 45–60 minutes.

2. **Add Salt & Oil** Add salt and olive oil. Mix well. Perform 3 stretch and folds over 1.5–2 hours.

3. **Bulk Fermentation** Let dough rest until puffed and airy (4–6 hours depending on your kitchen, or like me, skip this step and move straight to the next one.

4. **Layer & Roll** Turn out dough onto a floured surface. Gently press into a rectangle. Spread with cinnamon sugar mix, then roll up like a jelly roll.

5. **Pan & Cold Proof** Coil or gently twist the roll into a greased 9x13" baking tray or cast iron pan. Refrigerate overnight.

6. **Bake** The next day, remove from fridge and let rest at room temp while the oven preheats to 220°C (425°F). Bake 25–30 minutes until golden.

7. **Cool & Glaze** Let cool slightly, then drizzle with vanilla glaze.

This is incredible warm, especially with coffee. I recommend hiding a few pieces for yourself. You'll thank me later!

Sourdough Discard Ideas

Delicious Ways to Waste Less

If you've been feeding your starter regularly, you've likely noticed you end up with a fair bit of discard. And if you're anything like me, it feels a little wrong to toss something that smells so rich, alive, and full of potential.

The good news? You don't have to throw it out. Sourdough discard is one of the best "by-products" in your kitchen. Even though it's not quite strong enough to rise a full loaf on its own, it's still packed with flavour, natural fermentation benefits, and a beautifully tangy aroma that adds complexity to all sorts of baked goods.

This chapter is all about giving that discard a second life—and turning your scraps into something delicious.

What Is Discard, and When Can You Use It?

Sourdough discard is simply the portion of starter you remove before feeding. It still contains flour, water, and wild yeast, but its strength and activity vary depending on how recently it was fed.

You can use discard:

Straight from the fridge (if it's no more than 5–7 days old)

After a recent feed (but before it gets bubbly)

Mixed into recipes that use baking soda or baking powder as a rising agent

Don't use discard if:

It has a dark or pinkish tinge

It smells *genuinely* foul (think old socks or meat)

It has visible mold

When in doubt, trust your nose and instincts.

1. Fluffy Sourdough Discard Pancakes

These are a weekend favourite in my house. The discard adds a gentle tang that pairs beautifully with maple syrup or a dollop of coconut yoghurt.

Ingredients:

150g sourdough discard

150g all-purpose flour

1 tsp baking soda

1 tsp baking powder

1 tbsp sugar or maple syrup

1 egg (or egg replacer)

250ml milk or plant milk

1 tbsp melted butter or oil

Pinch of salt

Method:

1. Whisk wet ingredients (milk, egg, discard, oil).
2. In a separate bowl, combine flour, sugar, salt, baking soda, and powder.
3. Mix dry into wet just until combined.
4. Cook on a hot nonstick pan or griddle until golden on both sides.

I love to add fresh blueberries, sliced banana or chocolate chips right after pouring the batter onto the pan!

2. Cheesy Sourdough Discard Crackers

Crunchy, savoury, and super simple—these crackers are perfect with dips, soup, or just as a snack. Bonus: they store well in an airtight jar.

Ingredients:

100g sourdough discard

60g all-purpose flour

30g nutritional yeast (or grated parmesan)

1 tbsp olive oil

¼ tsp garlic powder

¼ tsp smoked paprika

½ tsp salt

Optional: sesame or poppy seeds for topping

Method:

1. Mix all ingredients into a dough (it'll be soft but workable).

2. Roll out thinly between two sheets of baking paper.

3. Score into cracker shapes.

   4. Bake at 170°C (340°F) for 15–20 minutes or until golden and crisp.

3. Quick Sourdough Discard Flatbread

This recipe is wonderfully forgiving. It's great for a weeknight wrap or as a quick side for soup or salad. I also use it to make delicious pocket style toasted sandwiches!

Ingredients:

200g sourdough discard

120g flour

1 tbsp olive oil

½ tsp salt

Optional: herbs, garlic powder, or za'atar

Method:

   1. Mix ingredients into a soft dough.

   2. Let rest for 15–30 minutes.

3. Divide into 4–6 pieces, roll out, and dry-fry in a hot pan for 1–2 minutes per side.

4. One-Bowl Sourdough Discard Banana Bread

Soft, rich, and with just a hint of tang—this banana bread is especially good with walnuts or a few dark chocolate chips tossed in.

Ingredients:

200g sourdough discard

2 very ripe bananas, mashed

100g sugar or coconut sugar

60ml oil or melted butter

1 egg (or egg replacer)

1 tsp vanilla

½ tsp baking soda

½ tsp cinnamon

200g flour

Pinch of salt

Method:

1. Mix everything in one bowl.

2. Pour into a greased loaf tin.

3. Bake at 175°C (350°F) for 45–55 minutes or until a toothpick comes out clean.

This also works as muffins; just bake 18–22 minutes instead.

Storage & Batch Tips

Discard can be stored in a sealed container in the fridge for up to a week.

Label it by date so you know what's still usable.

You can combine multiple days' worth for batch baking!

If you don't have time to use it, compost it, or share with a friend who bakes.

Final Thoughts

Using your discard isn't just economical, it's creatively satisfying. You're honouring the whole process, giving new life to something you might've thrown away, and adding even more nourishment to your table. It's one of those lovely reminders that sourdough, at its core, is about making the most of simple things.

Troubleshooting

Common Issues & Quick Reference Guide

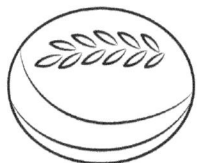

If your bread didn't turn out quite as expected, don't worry. Every loaf is a learning opportunity! Here are some common issues and how to fix them:

Dense Crumb: This could be due to under-fermentation. Make sure your dough is proofed enough before baking.

Flat Loaf: If your loaf spreads out instead of rising up, it may have over-proofed. Try shortening the proofing time next time.

Sticky Dough: Sourdough can be sticky! Wetting your hands can help, and remember that practice makes perfect.

Tough Crust: A rock-hard crust usually means too little steam in the oven. Try adding ice cubes or a tray of water to help your loaf stay moist during the first half of the bake.

Tears or Rips in the Dough: This can happen when the dough hasn't had enough time to rest or hydrate. Give it a little extra time before handling, and avoid overworking it during shaping.

Collapsed Loaf (After a Great Rise): This might mean the dough was over-proofed or handled too roughly when scoring or transferring. Be gentle and keep your final proof on the shorter side.

Starter Not Rising Well: If your starter is sluggish, try feeding it twice a day for a few days at room temperature. You can also switch up the flour or add a little whole wheat to boost activity.

Uneven Crumb or Large Holes at the Top: This often comes from shaping without enough surface tension, or from including too much air during folding. Focus on gentle shaping and good, even structure.

Every loaf teaches you something new, and the best way to learn is to keep baking, stay curious, be adventurous, and forgive the occasional floury flop! Your next loaf could just be the one that makes you fall completely in love with the process.

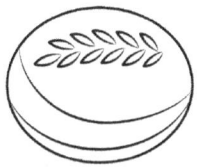

Basic Sourdough Baking Terms

Autolyse: Resting period where flour and water are mixed before adding salt and starter, helping gluten formation.

Bannetons: Baskets used for holding and shaping the dough during proofing.

Bulk Fermentation: Initial fermentation stage when the dough rises after mixing.

Crumb: The texture and pattern of holes inside the bread.

Fermentation: The process where yeast and bacteria produce gases, acids, and flavors.

Float Test: Method to check if the leaven is ready by dropping a small piece into water.

Hydration: The ratio of water to flour in a dough, impacting texture and crumb.

Leaven: A portion of mature starter mixed with water and flour to create a larger quantity for baking.

Oven Spring: Rapid rise in the oven due to heat expansion and steam.

Proofing: Final rise after shaping, also called the second fermentation.

Retardation: Slowing fermentation by refrigerating the dough for improved flavor.

Scoring: Slashing the top of the dough before baking to control the expansion and create decorative patterns.

Shaping: Forming dough into its final shape before the final rise.

Starter: A mixture of flour and water fermented with wild yeast and bacteria, used as a leavening agent.

Stretch & Fold or **Coil & Fold**: Technique to strengthen gluten structure by manipulating the dough during bulk fermentation.

Use this chart as a quick guide while you bake. Have fun and enjoy every moment of your sourdough journey!

Conclusion

Congratulations on baking your first (or fiftieth!) sourdough loaf, and thank you for joining me on this journey. Whether you came to sourdough seeking healthier options, a creative outlet, or just the simple joy of pulling a warm, crusty loaf from the oven, I hope this little guide has given you the confidence, clarity, and encouragement to keep going.

Sourdough is never just about the bread. It's about slowing down. Tuning in. Trying again. It teaches us patience and flexibility. It reminds us that even when something doesn't go perfectly, it can still turn out beautifully. Every loaf, lopsided or lofty, is a lesson in progress, not perfection.

With this revised edition, I've included some of the things that made my own baking more joyful over time:

New ways to **customise your bread with inclusions** like seeds, herbs, cheeses, or even fruit

Creative discard recipes that help you use every part of your starter and reduce waste

Extra tips and encouragement to help you troubleshoot and trust your instincts

I hope these additions help you feel even more equipped to experiment and make your sourdough journey your own. Maybe your next loaf will be loaded with toasted sesame seeds and smoked salt... or maybe you'll be flipping sourdough pancakes for Sunday breakfast. Either way, you're baking something real, something personal, and something nourishing.

So keep going. Keep experimenting. Keep trusting the process. And most of all, enjoy every step (and slice) along the way.

Happy baking!
Kate :)

CONCLUSION

About the Author

Kate Baker is a writer, mental health advocate, passionate home cook and former law enforcement officer who discovered the healing power of sourdough during some of the most challenging seasons of her life.

Throughout more than two decades in frontline policing, Kate used her love of cooking as a way to decompress, manage stress, and reconnect with peace and creativity. What began as a therapeutic ritual soon blossomed into a full-fledged passion, one that helped her navigate the long-term effects of PTSD, as well as a later diagnosis of a serious autoimmune condition. Baking, particularly sourdough, became more than a hobby; it became a way to nourish not just her body, but her spirit.

Like many instinctive cooks, Kate once believed sourdough was too technical or intimidating to master, but through a mix of curiosity, trial and error, and the magic of community-shared knowledge, she fell in love with the process. Her approachable, encouraging teaching style has helped hundreds of readers and viewers build confidence in their own kitchens, one loaf at a time.

Kate lives in New South Wales, Australia, with her wife and their endlessly opinionated cats. She is also the creator behind *Bakekat Kitchen*, where she shares simple, joy-filled recipes that are often gluten-light, dairy-optional, and always made with heart.

When she's not elbow-deep in dough, she's studying, enjoying the outdoors and writing about kindness, resilience, and the power of creativity to support emotional well-being. *Simply Sourdough* is her first cookbook – a love letter to everyone who's ever thought, "I could never bake that."

Spoiler: You absolutely can!

ABOUT THE AUTHOR

www.ingramcontent.com/pod-product-compliance
Lightning Source LLC
Chambersburg PA
CBHW052207090526
44583CB00017BA/2452